PARLIN MEMORIAL LIBRARY
EVERETT, MA

Biographies
Sieur de
LA SALLE

by Mary Englar

PARLIN MEMORIAL LIBRARY
EVERETT, MA

Consultant:
Melodie Andrews, PhD
Associate Professor of Early American History
Minnesota State University, Mankato

Capstone
press

Mankato, Minnesota

La Salle

Fact Finders is published by Capstone Press
151 Good Counsel Drive, P.O. Box 669, Mankato, Minnesota 56002
www.capstonepress.com

Copyright © 2005 by Capstone Press. All rights reserved.
No part of this publication may be reproduced in whole or in part, or stored in a retrieval
system, or transmitted in any form or by any means, electronic, mechanical, photocopying,
recording, or otherwise, without written permission of the publisher.
For information regarding permission, write to Capstone Press,
151 Good Counsel Drive, P.O. Box 669, Dept. R, Mankato, Minnesota 56002.
Printed in the United States of America

Library of Congress Cataloging-in-Publication Data
Englar, Mary.
   Sieur de la Salle / by Mary Englar.
   p. cm.—(Fact finders. Biographies)
   Includes bibliographical references (p. 31) and index.
   ISBN 0-7368-2666-1 (hardcover)
   1. La Salle, Robert Cavelier, sieur de, 1643–1687—Juvenile literature. 2. Explorers—
North America—Biography—Juvenile literature. 3. Explorers—France—Biography—
Juvenile literature. 4. Canada—Discovery and exploration—French—Juvenile literature.
5. Canada—History—To 1763 (New France)—Juvenile literature. 6. Mississippi River
Valley—Discovery and exploration—French—Juvenile literature. [1. La Salle, Robert
Cavelier, sieur de, 1643–1687. 2. Explorers. 3. Mississippi River—Discovery and
exploration. 4. America—Discovery and exploration—French.] I. Title. II. Series.
71030cbc.E54 2005
977'.01'092—dc22   2003023419

Summary: An introduction to the life of seventeenth-century French explorer René-Robert
   Cavelier, Sieur de La Salle, who explored the Great Lakes and the Mississippi River.

Editorial Credits
Roberta Schmidt, editor; Juliette Peters, series designer; Patrick Dentinger, book designer
   and illustrator; Erin Scott, Sarin Creative, map illustrator; Kelly Garvin, photo
   researcher; Eric Kudalis, product planning editor

Photo Credits
Art Resource, NY/Giraudon, 17
Corbis/Bettmann, 5, 13
Getty Images/Hulton Archive, 1, 14
National Gallery of Art, 20–21
North Wind Picture Archives, cover, 6–7, 8–9, 10, 11, 15, 18–19, 22–23, 25
Stock Montage Inc., 16
1 2 3 4 5 6 09 08 07 06 05 04

Table of Contents

Chapter 1

The Gulf of Mexico

On April 9, 1682, a small group of men in canoes reached the Gulf of Mexico. They had traveled all the way from the Great Lakes. Sieur de La Salle led the group. These men were the first Europeans to travel all the way to the mouth of the Mississippi River.

La Salle and his men went to shore. They planted a cross and pillar in the ground. The pillar had a design on it. The design was the **coat of arms** of Louis XIV, the king of France. La Salle **claimed** for France all of the land and rivers that touched the Mississippi River. He named this land Louisiana in honor of King Louis.

Sieur de La Salle (with sword) claimed for France a large piece of land he named Louisiana.

La Salle did not know the size of Louisiana. The land that he claimed stretched from the Appalachian Mountains to the Rocky Mountains. He had claimed the center of North America for France.

Chapter 2

A French Beginning

Sieur de La Salle was born in November 1643 in Rouen, France. His parents named him René-Robert Cavelier. His father, Jean Cavelier, owned a large piece of land called La Salle. René-Robert Cavelier became known as Sieur de La Salle. This title means "the gentleman from La Salle."

When La Salle was young, he went to a school run by Catholic **priests**. He studied religion, science, mathematics, and languages. La Salle learned quickly. When he was 17 years old, the priests asked him to join them. La Salle agreed. He gave up all of his money and property. He studied to become a priest.

La Salle was born in Rouen, France. Rouen was an important city along the Seine River.

After a few years, La Salle decided not to become a priest. He wanted to **explore** the world. He decided to travel to France's **colony** in North America, New France. La Salle sailed to New France in 1666.

Chapter 3

New France

In the mid-1600s, New France covered the eastern part of what is now Canada. It also included land around the Great Lakes.

In New France, La Salle traveled to Ville-Marie de Montréal. This town later became known as Montréal. Explorers and fur traders bought supplies there. Indians went there to trade beaver skins for French guns and tools.

The Europeans and Indians did not live together peacefully in New France. The Europeans pushed the Indians off of the land to start colonies. The Indians lost their homes and hunting grounds. Some of the Indians attacked the French colonies. The Indians tried to get their land back.

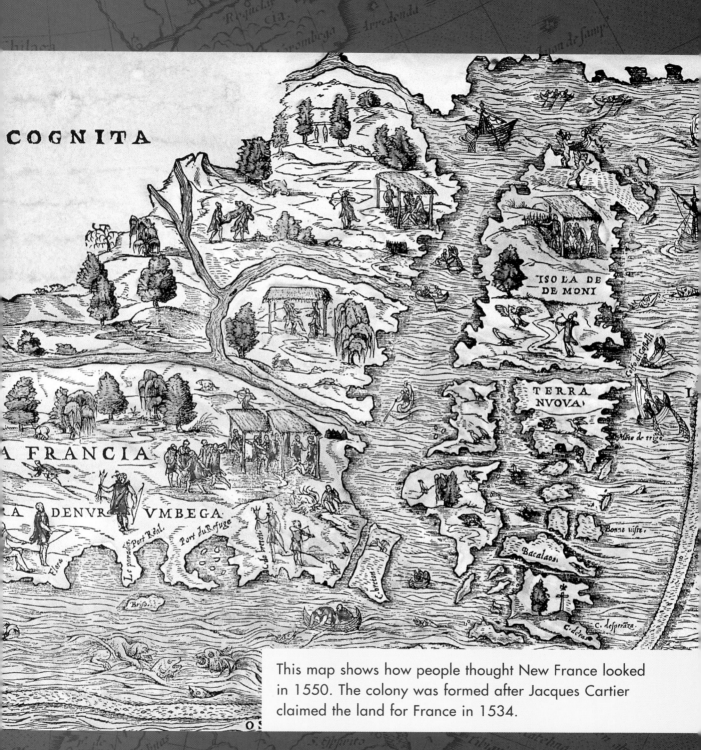

COGNITA

A FRANCIA

RA DENVR VMBEGA

ISOLA DE
DE MONI

TERRA
NVOVA

Bacalaos

This map shows how people thought New France looked in 1550. The colony was formed after Jacques Cartier claimed the land for France in 1534.

The fur trade was very important during La Salle's lifetime. Many Europeans wanted hats made out of fur. Fur traders in New France made a lot of money selling beaver skins for hats.

Many early French settlers ▼ were fur traders.

A New Home

The **colonists** of Montréal wanted more Europeans to settle in their town. They believed that more settlers could help protect against Indian attacks. They gave La Salle a large piece of land near the town.

La Salle became a fur trader. He often worked with Indians. La Salle learned a lot from these native people. They told him about the land. They also showed him how to hunt, paddle a canoe, and walk in deep snow with snowshoes.

▲ Fur traders often used the rivers to move their furs from place to place.

Rivers across North America

One winter, some Indians told La Salle about two large rivers. The Indians believed these rivers ran all the way to the ocean. La Salle decided to explore these rivers. He thought they might lead him to the Pacific Ocean. La Salle sold his land and bought supplies for an **expedition**.

Chapter 4

Early Expeditions

La Salle left Montréal in July 1669. He hired 14 men to travel with him. Several priests also joined La Salle. They wanted to teach their religion to Indians they met along the way. The group traveled with eight canoes.

The group crossed Lake Ontario and reached Lake Erie in September. In November, the group split up. Most of the men went back to Montréal. La Salle did not go with them. He did not return to Montréal until late 1670.

No one is sure where La Salle went during that year. Some historians believe he reached the Ohio River. He may have explored the river as far as present-day Louisville, Kentucky.

La Salle went on many expeditions between 1669 and 1680. His friends Henry de Tonti and Friar Louis Hennepin joined him on a few of the trips.

▲ La Salle traveled into the unknown lands beyond New France.

After La Salle returned to Montréal, he planned other expeditions. Over the next three years, he explored the unknown areas west and south of New France. By 1673, La Salle knew that the Ohio River did not reach the Pacific Ocean. But he was not ready to stop exploring.

La Salle learned about the journey of Jacques Marquette and Louis Jolliet. In the summer of 1673, these two French men had started to explore a great river that flowed south.

▲ Marquette and Jolliet explored part of the Mississippi River in 1673.

Indians called this great river the "father of waters." Today it is known as the Mississippi River. La Salle believed that this river flowed to the Gulf of Mexico.

La Salle decided to explore the Mississippi River. But first he had to make money for an expedition. He also needed permission from the king of France.

▲ King Louis XIV gave La Salle permission to explore the Mississippi River.

FACT!

The *Griffon* was the first ship to sail on the Great Lakes. It sank in a storm after La Salle reached Lake Michigan.

Forts and Exploration

In 1677, La Salle sailed to France. He asked King Louis for permission to explore the Mississippi River. The king agreed. He told La Salle to build **forts** for France during his explorations.

La Salle returned to New France in 1678. He helped build Fort Conti at the mouth of the Niagara River. He also continued to trade furs.

La Salle needed a large ship to carry furs to Montréal. In 1679, he built the *Griffon*. The *Griffon* was 50 feet (15 meters long). It could carry 45 tons (41 metric tons) of goods.

▲ La Salle built the *Griffon* in 1679.

La Salle sailed the *Griffon* to Lake Michigan. There, he built Fort Miami near present-day St. Joseph, Michigan.

In 1680, La Salle traveled down the Illinois River. He built another fort and called it Fort Crèvecoeur. The fort was near present-day Peoria, Illinois.

Chapter 5

The Mississippi Expedition

In December 1681, La Salle finally was ready to explore the Mississippi River. He gathered a small group of men for the expedition. His group included 23 French men, 18 Indians, and a priest.

The expedition started on the frozen Illinois River. The men had to pull their canoes over the ice. They reached the Mississippi River in February 1682. Ice still floated on the fast-moving water. La Salle and his men waited one week for the ice to melt. They then started to paddle down the Mississippi.

La Salle and his men explored from the Great Lakes to the Gulf of Mexico.

19

Indians

In March, La Salle and his group met some Arkansas Indians. These Indians were kind to the explorers. They invited La Salle and his men to their village. They gave them food and firewood. La Salle and his group stayed in the village for three days.

Before La Salle left, he set up a cross in the village. He claimed the land and the people for France.

The Arkansas Indians did not understand what La Salle was saying. They did not speak French. They had welcomed the explorers as friends. They had not agreed to give up their land or freedom.

This painting by George Catlin ➡ shows La Salle claiming the Arkansas Indians and their village.

The Gulf of Mexico

The explorers continued down the Mississippi River. On April 6, 1682, they reached a place where the river divided into three parts. La Salle sent canoes down each part. Soon, all of the canoes came to a large body of water. They had reached the Gulf of Mexico.

La Salle and his group paddled to the riverbank. The shore was covered with thick reeds. When the men stepped onto the land, they sank into mud. The explorers paddled back up the river until they found dry land.

La Salle set up a cross and pillar ➤ to claim the land for France.

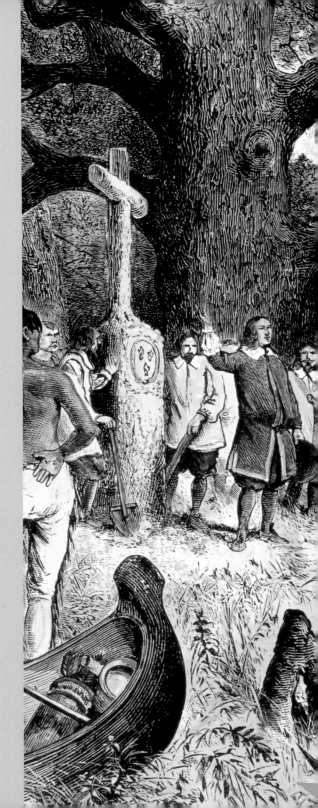

Louisiana

On April 9, 1682, La Salle claimed the land touching the Mississippi River for France. He also claimed all of the rivers that ran into the Mississippi and the land near them. La Salle named the land Louisiana, after King Louis.

La Salle and his group then started the long, hard journey back up the river. On the way back to New France, La Salle stopped along the Illinois River. He ordered the building of Fort St. Louis. The fort was built on a cliff now known as Starved Rock. This cliff is near present-day Utica, Illinois.

Chapter 6

The Last Expedition

La Salle sailed to France again in 1683. This time, King Louis gave La Salle permission to start colonies in Louisiana.

On July 24, 1684, La Salle left France with four ships and about 320 people. La Salle planned to start a colony at the mouth of the Mississippi River.

A few months later, the ships sailed into the Gulf of Mexico. La Salle looked for the Mississippi River. He could not find it. He took the ships too far west. Finally, in February 1685, La Salle and the colonists went to shore. They were in an area now known as Texas.

La Salle tried to start a colony in Louisiana. He instead ended up near Matagorda Bay, Texas.

25

La Salle's Death

By 1687, only 40 of the colonists were still alive. Many had died from disease. Others had been killed fighting Indians. But the survivors could not go back to France. All of the ships had sunk.

La Salle decided to get help. He took 20 men and set out for Montréal. They struggled through swamps and thick woods. The men were angry. On March 19, some of the men killed La Salle. They left his body in the woods.

Lasting Impact

Sieur de La Salle played an important part in the history of France and North America. La Salle's expeditions gave France a huge area of land in North America. He helped the world learn about the unknown lands around the Great Lakes and the Mississippi River.

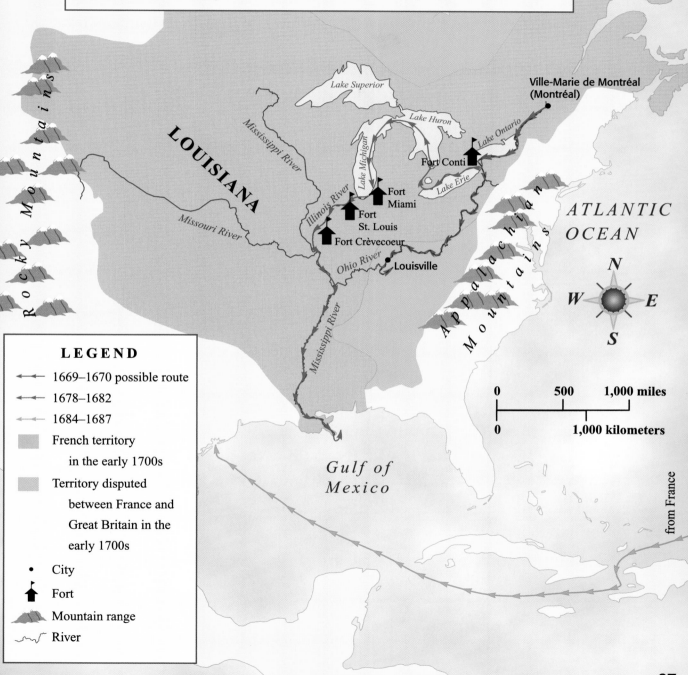

The Journeys of Sieur de La Salle, 1669–1687

Rocky Mountains

Lake Superior

Lake Huron

Lake Michigan

Lake Ontario

Ville-Marie de Montréal
(Montréal)

Mississippi River

LOUISIANA

Missouri River

Illinois River

Fort Conti

Lake Erie

Fort Miami

Fort St. Louis

Fort Crèvecoeur

Ohio River

Louisville

Appalachian Mountains

ATLANTIC OCEAN

Mississippi River

Gulf of Mexico

from France

LEGEND

- ←— 1669–1670 possible route
- ←— 1678–1682
- ←— 1684–1687
- French territory in the early 1700s
- Territory disputed between France and Great Britain in the early 1700s
- • City
- ⬆ Fort
- Mountain range
- River

N
W   E
S

| 0 | 500 | 1,000 miles |
| 0 | | 1,000 kilometers |

Fast Facts

- Sieur de La Salle's real name was René-Robert Cavelier. He was born in northern France.

- La Salle traveled down the Mississippi River and reached the Gulf of Mexico. He claimed the land for France and named it Louisiana.

- La Salle named Louisiana after the king of France, Louis XIV.

- La Salle got lost on his last expedition. He missed the mouth of the Mississippi River and landed in an area that today is the state of Texas.

- In 1995, scientists found the wreck of one of La Salle's ships. It was resting in Matagorda Bay on the Texas coast. La Salle had missed the Mississippi River by more than 400 miles (644 kilometers).

Time Line

Life Events of Sieur de La Salle

René-Robert Cavelier is born in Rouen, France. He is known as Sieur de La Salle.

La Salle explores the Mississippi River Valley. He claims it for France and names it Louisiana.

La Salle sails to New France.

La Salle is killed in Texas by his own men.

1541   1643   1666   1673   1681–1682   1687

World Events

Spanish explorer Hernando de Soto discovers the Mississippi River.

French explorers Jacques Marquette and Louis Jolliet travel down part of the Mississippi River.

29

Glossary

claim (KLAYM)—to say that something belongs to you or that you have a right to have it

coat of arms (KOHT UHV ARMS)—a design that stands for a family, city, state, or country

colonist (KOL-uh-nist)—a person who lives in a colony

colony (KOL-uh-nee)—an area that has been settled by people from another country; a colony is ruled by another country.

expedition (ek-spuh-DISH-uhn)—a long journey for a certain purpose, such as exploring

explore (ek-SPLOR)—to travel to find out what a place is like

fort (FORT)—a strong building used to protect people or places

priest (PREEST)—a member of a church who leads services and performs religious practices

Internet Sites

FactHound offers a safe, fun way to find Internet sites related to this book. All of the sites on FactHound have been researched by our staff.

Here's how:
1. Visit *www.facthound.com*
2. Type in this special code **0736826661** for age-appropriate sites. Or enter a search word related to this book for a more general search.
3. Click on the **Fetch It** button.

FactHound will fetch the best sites for you!

Read More

Bergen, Lara Rice. *The Travels of Sieur de La Salle.* Explorers and Exploration. Austin, Texas: Steadwell Books, 2001.

Donaldson-Forbes, Jeff. *La Salle.* Famous Explorers. New York: PowerKids Press, 2002.

Heinrichs, Ann. *La Salle: La Salle and the Mississippi River.* Exploring the World. Minneapolis: Compass Point Books, 2002.

Kline, Trish. *Robert La Salle.* Discover the Life of an Explorer. Vero Beach, Fla.: Rourke, 2002.

Index

PARLIN MEMORIAL LIBRARY
EVERETT, MA